The Riddle of the
Swastika

Servando Gonzalez

The Riddle of the
Swastika
A Study in Symbolism

To the memory of ManWoman (1936-2012), who devoted his
whole life to rescue the swastika for mankind.

El Gato Tuerto
Hayward, California

Prologue:

About 45 years ago, I gave a lecture on Communication Theory and Semiotics at the Lyceum Society in Havana. Though I mentioned many common symbols, however, maybe out of prejudice I did not mention a very important one.

After I finished my presentation, one of the persons who attended the lecture asked me about the swastika, and I gave a perfunctory answer in which I recall I mentioned that it was a very old symbol. I didn't know him at the time, but the person who asked me the question was Marcus Matterin, the Library Director at the Jewish Community Center in Havana. Later we became friends.

But he piqued my curiosity. Next day I went to the main library at the University of Havana where I discovered, to my total surprise, that in the 19th century already many articles and books had been written about the swastika. Actually, still the best works on the subject is *The Swastika: The Earliest Known Symbol* by Thomas Wilson, a curator at the U.S. National Museum of The Smithsonian Institution, who wrote his book in 1894, and *El Huracán: Su mitología y sus símbolos* (1947) by Cuban ethnologist Fernando Ortiz.

Since Matterin asked me that question I engaged in what I call "a search and rescue mission" of this symbol —which belongs to mankind, not to any particular ideology or political movement. But this ancient symbol has a very long and complicated history. What I will show you in this book is just the tip of the iceberg.

Servando Gonzalez

California, 2022.

Introduction

In modern times the swastika has been associated with evil

Adolf Hitler adopted it as a symbol of his Nazi movement

White separatists display it as a symbol of racial superiority

Charlie Manson had in tattooed on his forehead

But, what is the Swastika?

Is it a symbol of hate?

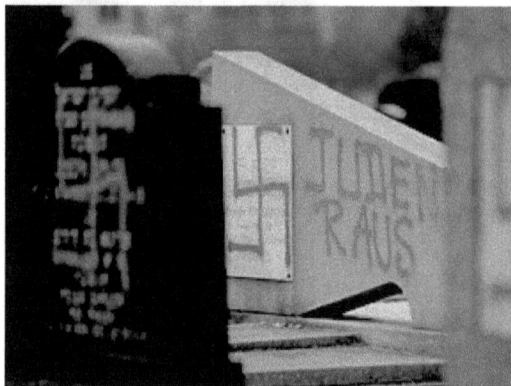

Jewish tombstones desecrated
with swastikas

or a symbol of love?

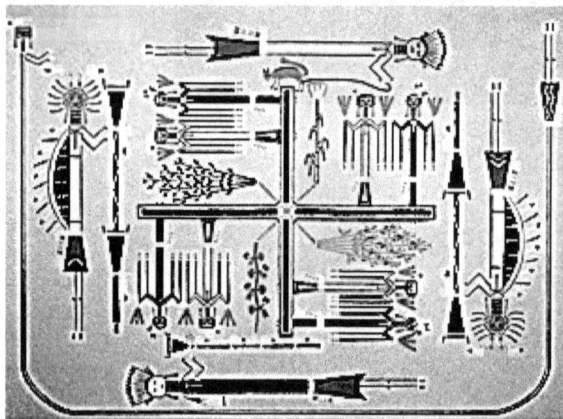

Swastika symbol on Navajo
sand painting

Pueblo Indian pottery rattle

A symbol of war?

American soldiers in WWII show captured Nazi Flag

Or a symbol of peace and good luck?

American good luck card

Swastika on Tibetan door as
a talisman for good luck

Around the world, the swastika has had many uses by different peoples

Communist Party electoral banner with hammer, sickle and swastika. Nepal, 1994

Some years ago, voters in Nepal went to the polls. They pressed their choice by stamping a swastika next to the name of the candidate of their preference.

The Kuna Indians in Panama design their *molas* (textile art) with colorful swastikas.

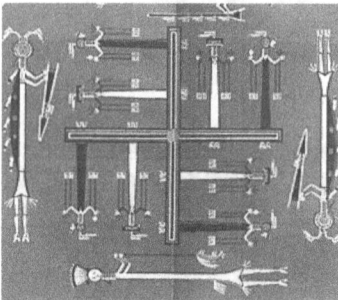

Navajo medicine men use colored sand to draw swastikas on the floor while performing their curative rites.

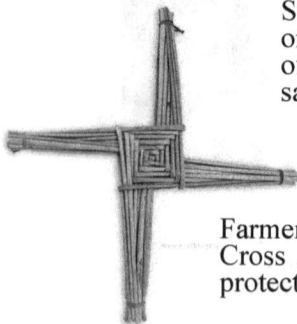

Swastikas are drawn on the shaved heads of Indian boys on sacred days.

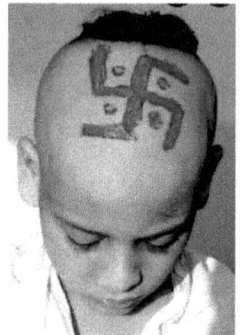

Farmers in Ireland place a Brigit Cross behind their main door to protect the house from evil spirits.

Now, we are about to begin a most fascinating journey.

A journey through the world of science, semiotics, anthropology and religion.

A journey through the world of myth, folklore, superstition and magic.

A journey through the world of evil and love.

A journey through the world of the oldest and most enigmatic symbols of mankind.

A journey through the world of the

swastika.

Part One
The Swastika and Its Names

Most researchers agree that he name swastika comes from the Sanscrit

Swastika

SUASTIKA:

A Sanskrit word composed of the adjective "su" = good, plus the verb "asti" = being (to be), followed by the substantival suffix, "ka" = it is.

Meaning, "It is (a) good (thing), i.e., as in "Good luck" (to you), or "May good luck attend you."

But around the world, the swastika has been known by different names in different cultures

Arani. A Hindu decorative motif of identical design and symbolism, and equally ancient and obscure in origin as the swastika.

Bride Baby. See Saint Brigid's cross.*

Celtic knot. Swastika-like designs commonly appearing in Celtic art in Scotland and Ireland.

Croce unicinate. Italian.

Croix a crochets. French.

Croix a virgules. Name given to the French Basque swastika. See Labaru.*

Croix Basque. French. name given to the Basque swastika.

Croix cantonée. See Croix swasticale.*

Croix cramponée. French. From its likeness to a metal cramp used in masonry.

Croix des Manichéens.

Croix du Verbe. French. Old Christian symbol formed by four gamma letters whose angles are turned towards the center. It represents Christ, and the gammas the four evangelists. See gammed cross.*

Croix gammée. French. (See Gammed Cross*)

Croix griffue. French.

Croix pattée. Legged cross. From the French.

Croix Potent. Cross terminating in crutchlike ends. Also cruckenkreuz.*

Croix swasticale. A Greek cross showing four dots on its intersection.

Cruckenkreuz.*

Crux adunca. Latin.

Crux decussata. Also called St. Andrews Cross.

Crux dissimulata. Early Christians used this named to designate the swastika, which they used as a disguised cross during the persecutions, hence this name.

Crux gammata. Latin. (See Gammed Cross).*

Crux Gothica. Also called running cross.

Crux Hermes.

Duck's wings. Name of a swastika-like design appearing in basketry of the Maidu Indians of California.

Flanged thwarts. A peculiar and most ancient mark in the form of a swastika.

Fylfot. Name said to have been derived from the Anglo Saxon "fower fot", meaning four-footed, or many-footed. According to some scholars, however, the word fylfot is of Scandinavian origin and is a compound of the old Norse "fiöl," or the Anglo-Saxon "fela," the German "viel," —English "full,"—and "fot", for foot —the many-footed figure.

Gammadion. See Gammed Cross*

Gammed cross. Cross formed by four gamma letters of the Greek alphabet.

Gyung-drung. Tibetan name for the swastika.

Haka Risti (locked cross). Light blue swastika, a traditional Lapp good-luck symbol.

Hakenkreuz. From the German: hooked cross

Hammarsmark. See Thor hammer's mark.*

Harvest Baby. See Saint Brigid's Cross.*

Hemera. Greek name for the swastika.

Jain cross. One of the names of the swastika in India. The Jain sect uses the swastika as an auspicious symbol connected with the seventh Jina.

Kruckenkreuz. Design combining the two possible virtual movements of the swastika; dextro-and sinistroverse. See croix potent.*

Labaru (laubaro). Basque, Spain swastika.

Lei wen. One of the names of the swastika in China.

Man. Name of the swastika on Buddha's breast.

Mang-ziou. One of the names of the swastika in Japan, meaning "the sign of 10,000 years".

Manji. One of the names of the swastika in Japan..

Mystic cross. A monogrammatic symbol formed by the combination of two syllables, su and ti —suti.

Mystic knot. An angular knot, or the mystic sign on the breast of Vishnu, being said to be a form of
the swastika.

Nandyavarta. Third sign of the footprint of Buddha.

Pentaskelion. From the Greek. Same symbol as the triskelion,* but five-legged.

Rebated Cross. Another name for the fylfot or swastika..

Running cross. Name used perhaps for its relation to the triskelion* and the tetraskelion.*

Saint Brigid's Cross. Ancient symbol still in use in some parts of Ireland and Scotland. Also known as "BrideBaby" or "Harvest Baby".

St. Andrews Cross. See Crux Decussata.

Sauvastika (suavastika). According to some scholars, Indian name for the sinistroverse swastika, the one running counterclockwise, i. e. with its legs pointing to the right.* If one accepts such hypothesis, the Nazi symbol was not a swastika, but a sauvastika.

Solomon's knots. Italian name for swastika-like designs also common in Celtic art.*

Part Two
The Swastika and Its Shapes

Around the world, the swastika has appeared in many shapes

dextroverse
(clockwise)

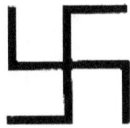

sinistroverse
(counterclockwise)

ogee

voluted

sigmoidean

circle-centered

spiral

circular

closed
meandroid

open
meandroid

North American

Basque

Jain

Angular

inverse

square-footed

tiled

superposed

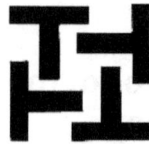

T-shaped

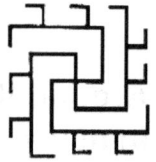

multi-legged

square-centered

quasi-swastika

labyrinthic

windmill

Celtic knot

Lapland

croix spatiale

dots-tipped

Tibetan

circle-tipped

off-centered

dextro-
sinistroverse

dotted

gammadion

continuous knot

croix
cramponée

anthropomorphic

zoomorfic

phytomorfic

short-legged

scandinavian

multilineal

human

angle-legged

moon-legged

Magatama

human

Arabic

Japanese

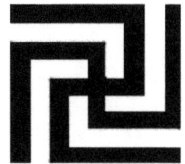

Greek

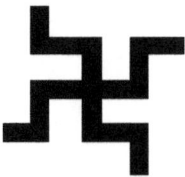

Balinese

Celt

Triskelion

Part Three
The Swastika Around the World

Ancient swastikas appear all around the world, except in Australia. The oldest examples have been found in the Caucasus mountains, dating from five to seven thousand years B.C.

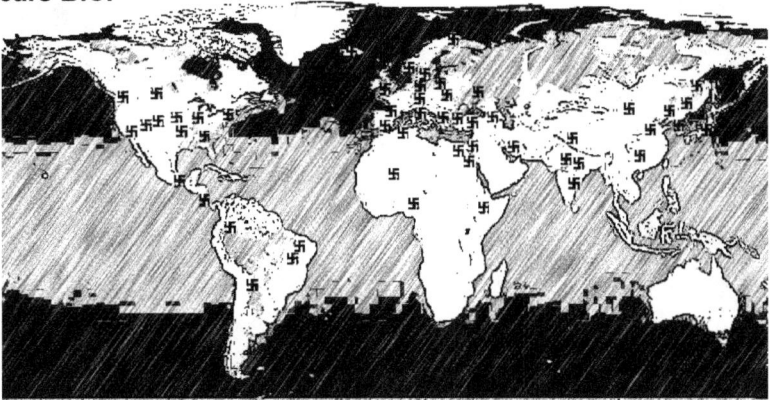

The position of the swastikas on the map is approximate

North America

Fragment from shell gorget found in Tennessee.

Clay vessel. Arkansas.

Wolpi Indians shaker. From New Mexico.

Clay Bowl. Mississippian period (1200-1600 AC)

Cherokee basket.
Oklahoma.

Zuni clay bowl. Arizona.

Clay pot. Mississippi
River valley.

Navajo sand painting.
Arizona

Swastika engraved in prehistoric ruins.
Cañon del Muerto, a branch of the Cañón de Chelly in the
Navajo reservation in St. Michael's. Arizona.

Pima basket design.
Arizona.

Zuni red ware clay
bowl. Arizona.

Navajo clay
bowl. Arizona.

Black clay bottle.
Louisiana.

Hammered copper symbols.
Hopewell, Ohio.

Stamped pottery vessel
Found near Horseshoe, Florida.

Central America

Design on flat clay stamp.
Nayarit, Mexico.

Design on flat clay stamp.
Found at State of Mexico.

Design on flat clay stamp.
Guerrero Mexico.

Bone stamp from
Xochimilco, Mexico D.F.

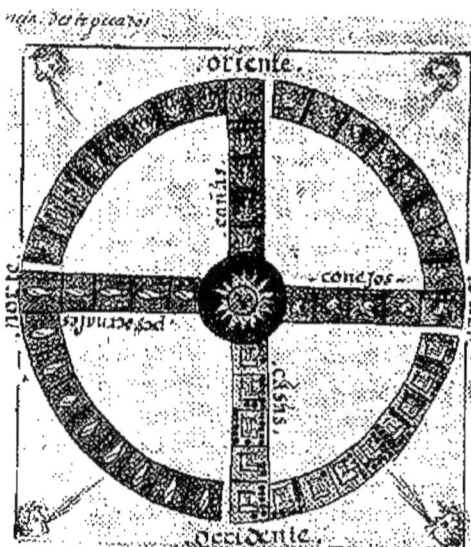

Aztec calendar as circular-shaped swastika.
From an Aztec codex (painted book).

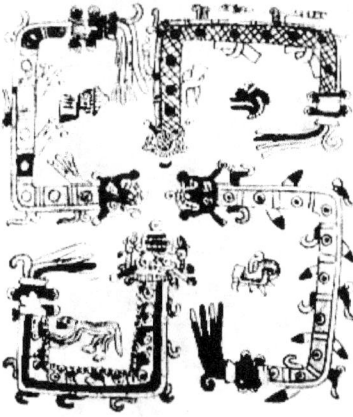

Swastika formed by four feathered
serpents of god Quetzalcoatl.
From Aztec codex.

Maya engraving on rock of god
Kukulkan with two overlapping
swastikas in the background.

Quiche-Maya design
from Tabasco. Mexico.

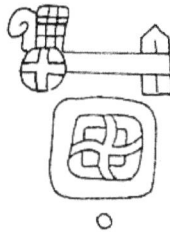

Year design from Monte
Albán, near Oaxaca.

Swastika design from
Teotihuacán. Toltec.

Stone lintel with swastika design.
Mixtec culture. Oaxaca, Mexico.

Kuna basket. Gulf of
San Blas, Panama.

Kuna mola. Gulf of
San Blas, Panama.

Hollow red ware Whistle
from Costa Rica.

Stone work on gravestone
from Costa Rica.

South America

Baniva pottery.
Amazonia, Brazil.

Engraving on rock.
Tiahuanacu, Peru.

Panobo polychrome
pottery. Amazonia, Brazil.

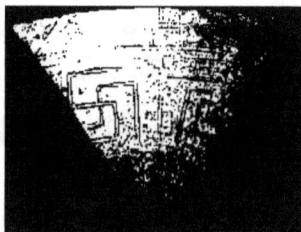

Terracotta cover "tanga."
Caneotires river, Brazil.

Europe

Bronze shield
(Battersea Shield)

Detail shows 9 squared-footed swastikas. This bronze shield with colored glass inlays was recovered from the River Thames at Battersea, London, in 1857.

Celtic carved cross with swastikas, in Carew, Pembrokeshire, U.K.

Triskelium (three-legged swastika). Symbol of Mannanan, sea god patron of the Isle of Man.

Asia

Detail of the Diamond Sutra, the oldest printed book,
dated 868 A. D. It shows Buddha
with a dextroverse swastika on his chest.

Tibetan Wheel of Law
with triskelium, swastika.

Large vase with swastikas at the
Senso-Ji temple, Tokyo, Japan.

South Asia

Second Century B.C. coin.
Kulutas tribe, Punjab, India.

Votive clay relief. India.

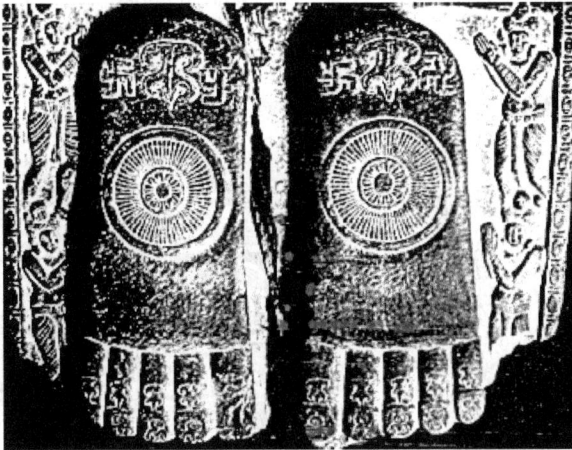

Footprints from the Buddha. 2nd. Century A.D.
Amaravatu, India.

Many clay seals like these, dated second o third millennium B.C.,
have been found in the ruins of the Harappan culture. India.

Africa

Ashanti gold weight.
Ghana.

Swastika in sunken church
of St. Mary. Ethiopia

Middle East

Mosque, Iran, 12th century.

6th century house. Ctesiphon, Iraq.

Floor mosaic, Jordan.

Carved panels, Great Mosque
of Kairowan, Jordan.

Decorative relief at
Baram synagogue

Decorative lintel at synagogue.

Carved stone lintel with dextro- and sinistroverse
swastikas. From synagogue at Capernaum.

Carved stone with swastikas from
synagogue at Capernaum.

Part Four
Origins and Antiquity

Figurine carved on ivory.

Engraved ivory bracelet.

The bird ivory figurine above is from Mezin, a little village on the Desna River, Ukraine, believed to have been made in the Upper Paleolithic, 18,000 to 15,000 B.C. The bracelet (bracelit) is also from Mezin,. Also believed to be made 18,000 to 15,000 B.C.

Samarran pottery bowl. Iraq.

Fragment of bronze belt. Bronze age.

One of the earliest swastikas known is painted on a Samarra (Iraq) pottery bowl dating to about 4,000 B.C. The bronze belt fragment is dated ca. 1100 to 400 B.C. Found at the Bronze Age Necropolis of Koban, central Caucasus.

Mohenjo-daro clay seal.

Harappan clay seals.

Engraved stone at
Ikely Moor, England.

Engraved stone at Gulfoes, Portugal.

The swastika was commonly used as a symbol in ancient Greece.
The Lady of the Beasts, surrounded by animals and swastikas
was a common theme in Beotian amphoras of 700 B.C.

In Rome the swastika was commonly used just as decoration, as in this frieze on the Ara Pacis, or Alexander the Great's sarcophagus.

It was also used as an early Christian symbol in the Roman catacombs.

Part Five
The Swastika in the Physical World

Swastikas in the physical world around us

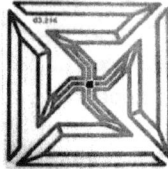

The swastika may appear spontaneously in the physical world, as in this expressway crossing near Los Angeles, in a hand knot, and in a computer chip.

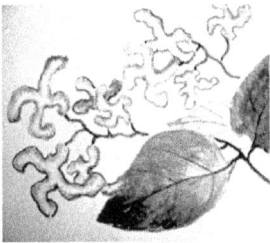

It can also appear naturally, as in a Chinese wild date fruit, a flower, the left ventricle of a sheep's heart, in an Airis spiral, a magnetic field, and in a tropical hurricane.

Swastikas in the microworld

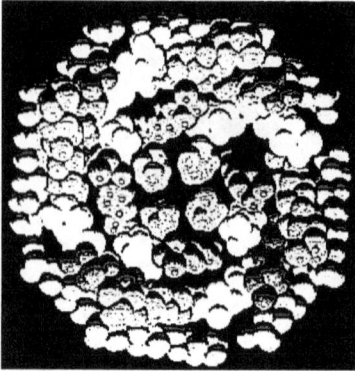

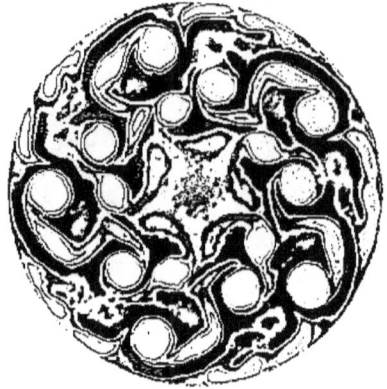

Swastikas appear in the microworld, as in this representation on the left of a sodium channel, a large protein embedded in the membrane of nerve cells. It also appears in the form of a five-legged sinistroverse pentaskelion in this experiment of miniature storms created by physisist Robert Ecke at the Los Alamos National Laboratory in New Mexico. (*Discovery* magazine, July 1993, p. 12)

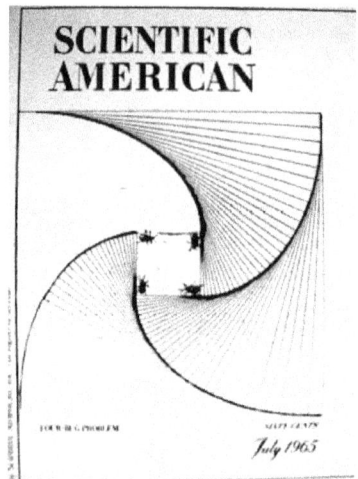

A swastika appears in the spatiotemporal pattern of calcium activity, as observed by confocal microscopy, as depicted in the cover of *Science* magazine on April 5, 1991. It also appears in the representation of the mathematical 4 bugs problem, which appeared on the cover of *Scientific American* on July, 1965.

Swastikas in the macroworld

Galaxy Mercier 101 in the form of an almost perfect sinistroverse sigmoidean swastika.

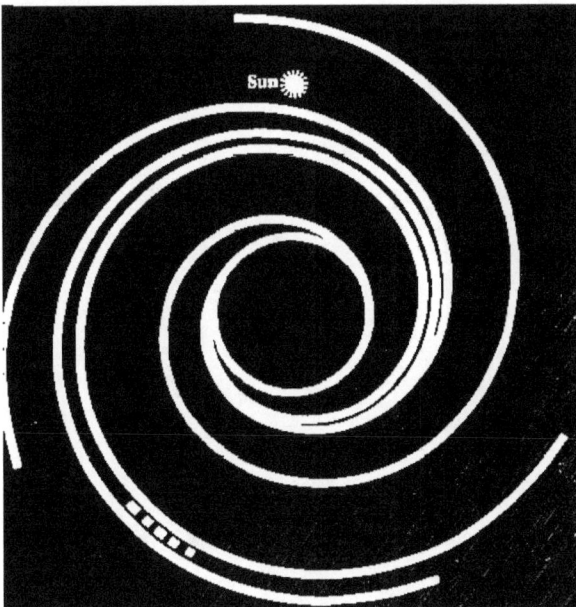

Graphical representation of the Milky Way, our own galaxy, as a dextroverse sigmoidean triskelion.

Part Six
The Swastika's Virtual Movement

The Swastika evidences a virtual movement, rotating around its center

CLOCKWISE
DEXTROVERSE

COUNTERCLOCKWISE
SINISTROVERSE

The picture on the left represents the virtual movement of the swastika as I have used it throughout this book. As I mentioned before, however, there is no agreement among the scholars who have studied this symbol about which one should be called a clockwise, dextroverse swastika and which one a counter-clockwise, sinistroverse one.

It supports my usage the fact that both Robert Wilson, in his book *The Swastika* (1894), as well as noted Cuban ethnologist Fernando Ortiz in his book *El Huracán* (1947), share this interpretation. Still, there is more evidence supporting this view.

The virtual movement of the swastika is depicted in the above illustration, a cover of a fireworks box from India (c. 1930). As it is shown in the picture of the swastika wheel on the upper right corner, once ignited the swastika will turn counterclockwise, that is, contrary to the direction of its arms.

But the fact that the virtual movement of the swastika runs in the opposite direction of its arms, has been a source of confusion. Author Rudiger Dahle has suggested to visualize it with its legs ended in four flame throwers, creating a jet flow to better evidence the direction of the swastika's virtual movement.

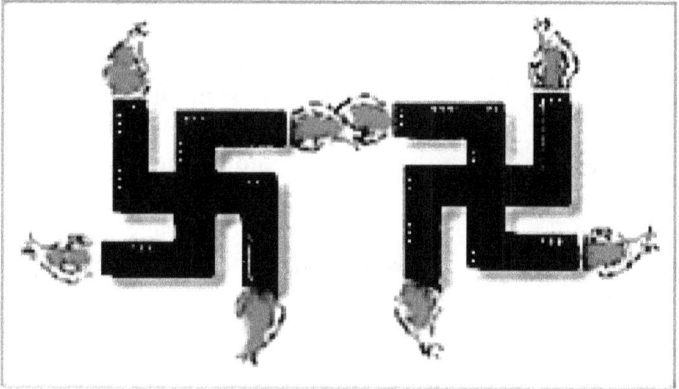

Rudiger Dahle, Mandalas of the World (New York: Sterling Publishing, 1992), pp 90-91.

Moreover, one of the meanings of the swastika around the world is axial rotation or circular movement, better seen in the sinistroverse spiral swastika seen below.

Unfortunately, however, approximately half of the books about the swastika explain it the other way around. Why do I think the explanation I have illustrated above is the right one?

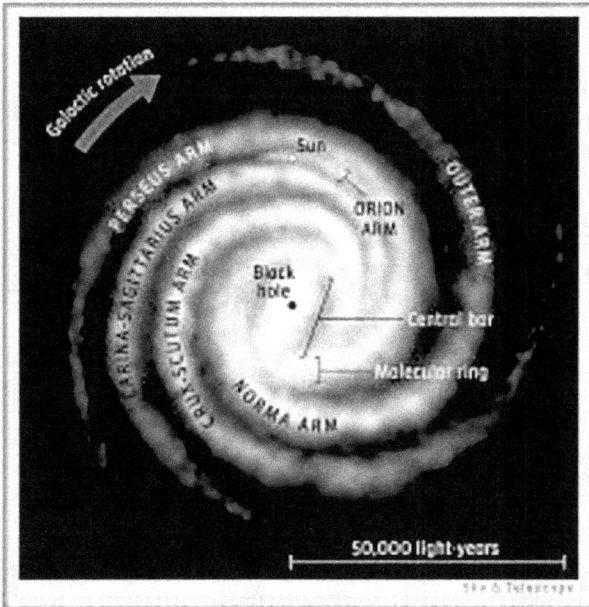
Spyral galaxy

Tropical hurricane

Both spyral galaxies and tropical hurricanes rotate from the arms towards the center, not the other way around.

Most simple geometrical forms —a square, a triangle, a circle—don't change when flipped on its vertical axis, but the swastika does. This phenomenon is called *chirality*.

An object is chiral when it is distinguishable from its mirror image, that is, it cannot be superimposed to it.

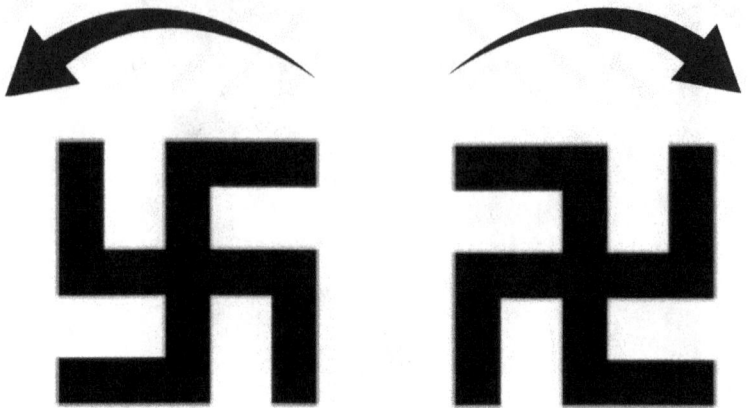

Swastika's virtual axial rotation

counter clockwise
left-turning
sinistroverse

clockwise
right-turning
dextroverse

The tendency to connect the left with evil is very old. When the Babylonians drew omens they usually considered the left side bad and the ride side good. In Homer birds flying towards the right are a favorable omen, while the ones flying to the left are unfavorable Sinister is the Latin word for both left and evil, a meaning still kept in English and in most romance languages.

The left has always been associated with evil. Black magic is also called "the Left-hand Path." Moving to the left in magic is always done with evil intent and it is supposed to attract evil influences. Some spells work only if you move to the left while repeating them. Thus the origin of the word "sinister."

According to some scholars, "swastika" is properly the name for the symbol running dextroverse or clockwise, i. e. with its legs pointing to the left, while the sinistroverse swastika would properly be a sauwastika.

Part Seven
The Swastika and its Symbolism

Since ancient times, the swastika has been used as an ornament, as an amulet, as a talisman and as a symbol.

The Swastika as an ornament

Greek frieze

Egyptian frieze

The swastika as an ornamental frieze decorating buildings is very common all around the world. In America, the best example of this is in the U.S. Capitol building in Washington, D.C.

The Swastika as a talisman

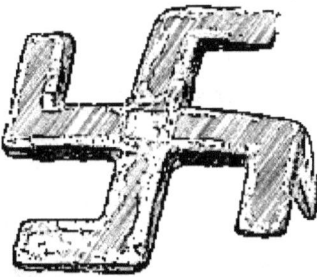

Roman fibula (brooch)

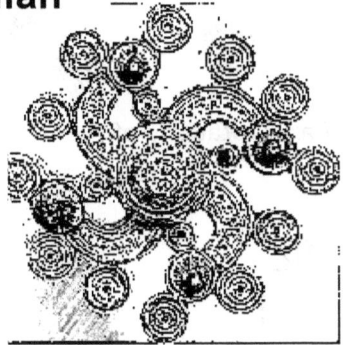

Scandinavian fibula

The swastika has also been used as a talisman, an object that has magical powers or exerts magnetic or psychic influences. Contrary to the amulet, who has intrinsic magical powers, a talisman needs to be "charged" with these powers and has an specific use, like making money, getting a job or conquering a woman.

The Swastika as an amulet

Brigit's cross

Good Luck coin

The Swastika as a symbol

of axial rotation

of the sun wheel

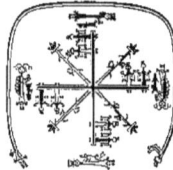

of the four seasons

of war

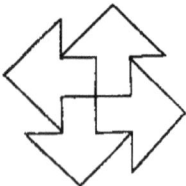

of lightning

of fertility

of speed

But one of the most known uses of the swastika is perhaps as a symbol of Nazism. But, what is a symbol? In order to understand what a symbol is, we need to take a look at Semiotics, the science that studies symbols.

Part Eight
The Science of
Semiotics

Every thing around us emits its particular physical signal that excites our senses: sound, smell, movement, light ...

But we can react only to a few of the thousands of signals that pour in upon our senses from all directions

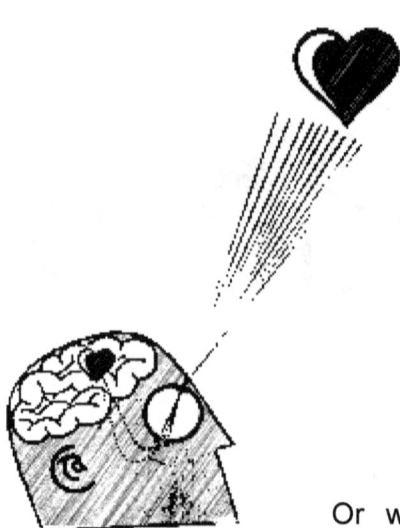

We can interpret things just as what they are.

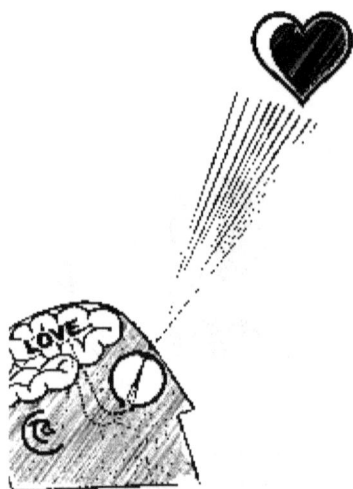

Or we can interpret them as quite different things. When this happens, we are interpreting things as *signs* of quite different things.

The process of interpreting things as signs is called *semiosis*, and the science that studies this process is called *semiotics*.

The science of semiotics was independently created both by Swiss linguist Ferdinand de Saussure and American philosopher Charles Sanders Peirce.

Saussure specialized in linguistic semiotics, and Pierce in visual semiotics —that's the one we will discuss here.

Ferdinand de Saussure

SEMIOTICS:

Charles Sanders Peirce

Semiosis:

The process by which something acts as a sign for somebody.

—Peirce

According to Peirce, a sign is something that stands to somebody as something else in some respect or capacity. Keep in mind that things are things. It is only when somebody takes them for another thing that they become signs. Like beauty, signs are in the eye of the beholder. This explains why the same thing can be interpreted differently by different people.

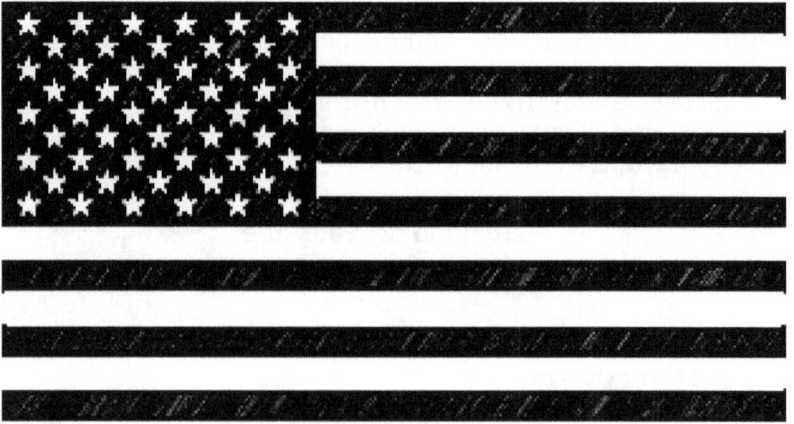

If somebody sees this object as a piece of cloth of different colors, there is no semiosis in it. If somebody sees it as a symbol of America, semiosis have occurred.

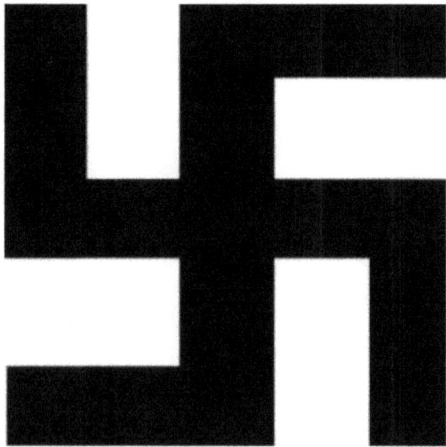

If somebody sees this object as a vertical line crossed by a horizontal one, with four smaller lines attached at an angle to its extremes, there is no semiotic process involved. If somebody sees it as a symbol of love or a symbol of hate, semiosis has occurred.

Peirce classified signs into three different categories:

**indexes,
icons and
symbols**

Charles P. Peirce

Indexes

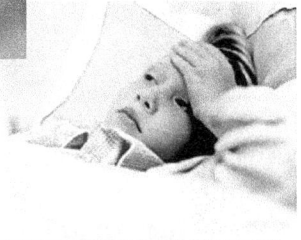

An index is a sign directly related, mostly by cause to effect, or antecedent to consequent, to what it signifies.

To Robinson Crusoe, footprints on the beach were an index that somebody had visited the island. High fever is an index of disease. Dark clouds are a sure index of a coming storm.

Icons

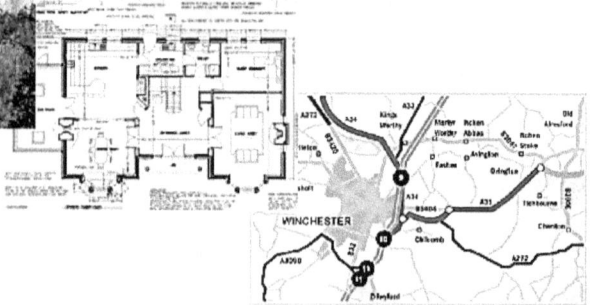

An Icon is a sign that represents its objet by visually resembling it. The image showing on the TV is an iconic sign of the boy. Photographs, diagrams, plans and maps are iconic signs. (Ansel Adams' Yosemite photo).

Belgian surrealist painter René Magritte expressed it beautifully in his 1929 painting "The Treachery of Images," which he cryptically subtitled "*This is not a pipe.*"

Ceci n'est pas une pipe.

Magritte was right. That is not a pipe you can put tobacco on its chamber and smoke it. It is just a picture, that is, an iconic representation of a pipe.

Symbols

A symbol is a type of sign that shows no relationship whatsoever between itself and what it signifies. The connection is established not because of cause-effect or likeness, but because a convention accepted by a group of individuals. Contrary to indexed and icons, which mostly can be intuitively decoded, symbols must be learned.

The meaning attached to a symbol is not the result of any causal connection with the thing symbolized, but the product of a convention or agreement.

Part Nine
The Nazis and the Swastika

The most widely accepted explanation of how Adolf Hitler adopted the swastika as a symbol of the Nazi movement is found in his *Mein Kampf*. The connection, he claimed, came through Dr. Friedrich Krohn, a dentist, and member of the Nazi party.

Yet, as many things related to Hitler and the Nazis, there are other plausible explanations. This study is an attempt to bring some light to other not so well known connections. These con- nections are not presented in order of importance, nor are they exhaustive.

The Khron Connection

Dr. Friedrich Khrohn

In *Mein Kampf*, Adolf Hitler claimed that the form in which the Nazis used the swastika was based on a design by Dr. Friedrich Krohn, a dentist who had belonged to several Völkisch groups, including the Germanen Order.

Krohn, a dentist from Starnberg, submitted his design of a flag which had been used at the founding meeting of his own party local: a swastika against a black-white-red back-ground.

Hitler gave his own account:

Actually, a dentist from Starnberg did deliver a design that was not bad after all, and, incidentally, was quite close to my own, having only the one fault that a swastika with curved legs was composed into a white disk.

Krohn knew that the Buddhist destroverse or clockwise swastika symbolized good fortune and well being, and made his design accordingly, with the swastika's legs pointing to the left.

The majority of the Nazi leaders accepted Krohn's design, but Hitler insisted on a sinistroverse or anti-clockwise swastika and changed the design, similar to the one on the right.

Adding credibility to this theory is the fact that the Nazis went to extremes to guarantee that the swastika on their banners and flags always appeared in its sinistroverse, counterclockwise form.

This is evidenced in the official Nazi specs for the construction of the Nazi flag. The Nazis went to great lengths to avoid that, by transparency, their swastika may appear dextroverse on one side. That's why it requires two circular pieces of white cloth attached at both sides of the red cloth, and two different sinistroverse swastikas attached at both sides, so that, from both sides, the Nazi flag will show a sinistroverse swastika.

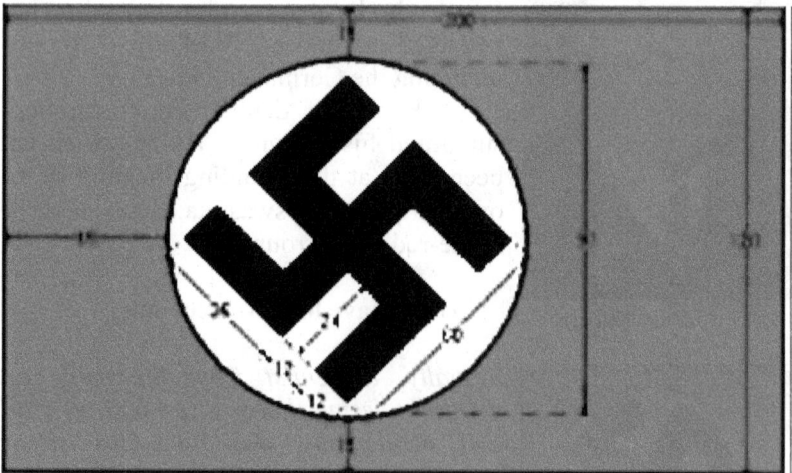

It is also believed that it was Hitler's idea to depict the swastika lying on an angle, because this added dynamism to the virtual rotation of the symbol.

The Haushofer Connection

Karl Haushoher

Notwithstanding Adolf Hitler's claims to the contrary, some authors believe that it was Karl Haushofer, whom they see as Hitler's guiding brain, the one who suggested to the Führer the adoption of the swastika as the Nazi symbol.

Haushofer was known to have had a reputation for precognition, manifested when he was a young field artillery officer in the Bavarian army. In 1908 the army sent him to Tokyo to study the Japanese army and to advise it as an artillery instructor. The assignment During his stay in the Far East he was introduced to Oriental esoteric teachings and became an authority in Oriental mysticism. Some authors even believe that he was the leader of a secret community of initiates in a current of Satanism through which he sought to raise Germany to world power, though these occult connections have been denied

It is also believed that he belonged to the esoteric circle of George Gurdjieff. Others claim that he was a secret member of the Thule Society. Some authors have linked Haushofer's name with another esoteric group, the Vril Society, or Luminous Lodge, a secret society of occultists in pre-Nazi Berlin.

As a professor at Munich University Haushofer developed new doctrine he calle geopolitics. Among his students was a young, bright army officer named Rudolf Hess who became Haushofer's favorite student. Later Hess also became one of the closest associates of Hitler. It was Rudolf Hess who introduced Haushofer to Adolf Hitler, Haushofer frequently visited the Führer while he was writing *Mein Kampf*.

Rudolf Hess

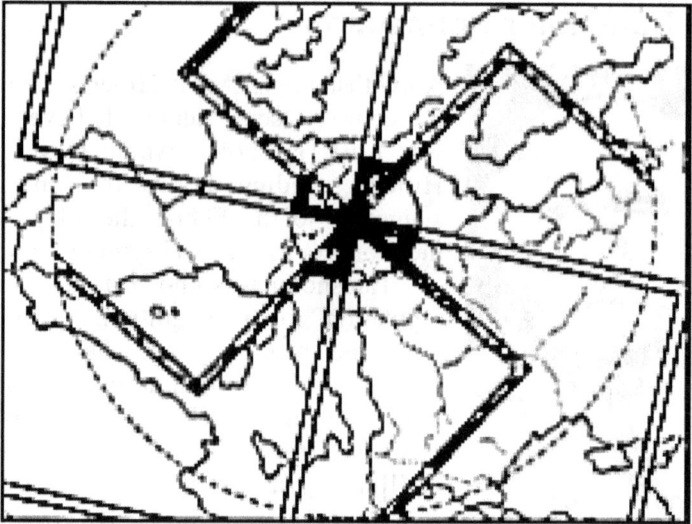

According to some sources, Haushofer advised Hitler to enlarge the living space of the Third Reich by moving out to a powerful territorial hub and by accomplishing this conquest progressively, step by step, following the accelerating movement of a growing sinistroverse swastika.

The Lambach Connection

Other authors believe that Hitler's first contact with the swastika began a long time before, while he was a young student with the Benedictines at the Abbey of Lambach-am-Traum, in upper Austria, where it had been sculpted several years before following orders from the Abbot, Theodorich Hagen.

At the Lambach Abbey young Adolf Hitler must have seen the swastika on the monastery.

In 1856 Father Hagen made a long trip to the Near East visiting, among other places, Persia, Arabia, Turkey, and the Cau-casus. Upon his return to Lambach in 1868 he hired workers and cabinet makers, whom he ordered to sculpt the swastika (on stone and wood) on the four corners of the building,

The Hess Connection

Like Adolf Hitler, Rudolf Hess always felt strongly attracted by the occult. He volunteered for the army and became an officer. When WWI ended he went to Munich and joined the Thule Society. He was only 22.

Hess was one of the hundreds of war veterans recruited in Munich by Baron von Sebottendorf to join the Freikorps.   Later Hess joined the German Workers Party.

It was in one of its meetings where he saw Adolf Hitler for the first time and was instantly captivated by Hitler's charismatic powers. When the would-be Führer ended his inflammatory speech, Hess was already one of Hitler's close followers.

Hess (second from right) with Hitler at Landsberg

A few months later, Hess became Hitler's personal secretary. With Hitler, he participated in the failed Munich Beer Hall putsch of 1923. He escaped to Austria, but when Hitler was sent to prison he gave himself up to the authorities to join the Führer at the Landsberg prison, where he helped Hitler in writing *Mein Kampf.*

Some people believe that Hess was instrumental in Hitler's decision of adopting the swastika as the Nazi symbol.

The Ehrhardt Brigade Connection

The Ehrhardt Brigade, was led by former captain Hermann Ehrhardt. In 1920, he chased the Reich government out of Berlin, until a general strike put down the military putsch. When the Ehrhardt Brigade marched into Berlin, its soldiers sported on their steel helmets a symbol they had brought from the battles in the Baltic. As they swung along, the Ehrhardt soldiers sang their marching song:

> Swastika on helmets,
> Colors red-white-black,
> The Ehrhardt Brigade,
> Is marching to attack!

It is interesting to notice that he Ehrhardt Brigade sported the swastika both in its dextroverse and sinistroverse forms lying flat on its side, while the Nazi swastika, following Hitlers specific instructions, appeared only in its sinistroverse form, lying vertically on one of its angles.

The Wagner Connection

Richard Wagner

Wagner was a sort of catalyzer in the resurgence of the swastika.

According to Hitler's friend August Kubizek, it all began at the opera on an evening of November 1906, after they have just heard Richard Wagner's Rienzi. After the performance they walked out of the city and climbed to the top of a hill where Guido von List had planted empty bottles in the form of a swastika. Once there, his eyes shining with excitement, Hitler began talking as if possessed by an invisible force.

Hitler claimed that his worldview had been inspired by Wagner. His youthful reaction to Wagner's opera Rienzi led him to exclaim 30 years later: "It all began at that hour." In *Mein Kampf*, he praised Wagner as a great revolutionary and claimed to have no forerunner except Wagner.

Indeed, the works of Wagner gave the swastika the necessary musical impetus for its resurgence with all the strength of old myths and legends.

The von List Connection

Guido von List

As early as 1875, Guido von List, a poet and nationalist ideologue, became so fascinated with ancient runes and symbols that, on the sunrise of the summer solstice, he walked up a hill near Vienna with a backpack full of empty wine bottles. Once on top of the hill, he buried the bottles in the shape of a swastika to celebrate the longest day of the year.

Hitler's friend Kubizek recalled that, after seeing Wagner's Rienzi, Hitler fell in a sort of trance, and walked up the hill to contemplate the bottles in the shape of a swastika List had buried. Hitler was so intrigued by List's burial that he wanted to exhume this 'first swastika' once he had annexed Austria.

List suggested the swastika as a symbol for all anti-Semitic groups. According to List, the swastika was the symbol of a secret group of initiates called the Armanen or "children of the sun," who had flourished in ancient times.

According to List the Armanen alone possessed the "secret of power." According to him, the Armanen, who had been forced underground by Christianization, had passed down the "secret of power" to the present day through secret brotherhoods. This "original knowledge" or "universal knowledge" of the Armanen, List believed had been retained in the secret societies of the Templars, Johanniter Order, Rosicrucians and Freemasons.

THE RELIGION OF THE
ARYO-GERMANIC FOLK

ESOTERIC AND EXOTERIC

GUIDO VON LIST

The Rosenberg Connection

Alfred Rosenberg

Among the many people who may have influenced Adolf Hitler's in the selection of the swastika as a Nazi symbol was Alfred Rosenberg, who some called the "intellectual leader" of the Nazi movement. Despite his Jewish origins, Rosenberg gained access to the exclusive Thule Society where he met Rudolf Hess, Dietrich Eckart and other high-rank Nazi members

Rosenberg with Hitler

After the creation of the Nazi Party Eckart introduced Rosenberg to Adolf Hitler, and the young Jewish German emigré from Russia became an active Party member. In 1930 Ro- senberg reached a high point in his career as a Nazi ideologue with the publication of his most important work, *The Myth of the 20th Century*.

According to a review of that time, Rosenberg's book was, "with Hitler's *Mein Kampf*, the most important work on National Socialism." The book eventually became a best seller, and sold more than one million copies.

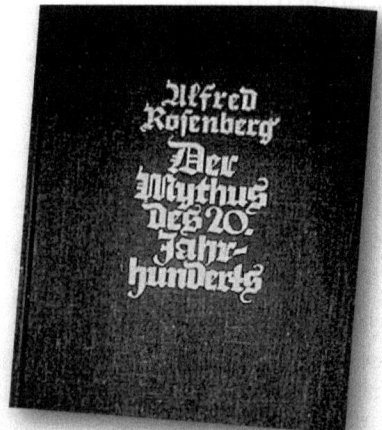

During World War II, Rosenberg led an art looting group which carried off to Germany more than 21,000 carloads of stolen paintings, rare books, sculptures, and jewelry. Much of this loot found its way into the private collections of Reichmarshall Herman Göering. Anxious to be in Hitler's good graces, some Nazi leaders, Rosenberg prominently among them, repudiated Christianity completely. Instead, they wanted to set up a pagan cult of "blood, race, and soil." They would go back to the dark ritual of dramatic rites of their ancestors, which they called "The New Pagans."

The New Pagans resurrected Odin, Thor, and the old gods of primitive Teutons before Christ's time. Instead of the Old Testament they adopted Nordic sagas, fairy tales and the swastika as a symbol of the Nazism. They set up a new trinity for worship — bravery, loyalty, and physical force.

The time of the Cross has gone now,
The Sun-wheel shall arise,
And so, with God, we shall be free at last
And give our people their honor back.

In 1937, Hitler awarded the National Prize, Germany's version of the Nobel Prize, to Alfred Rosenberg, maximum foe of Christianity and leader of the New Pagans. Rosenberg, the Jew turned into Nazi philosopher, wanted a return to the old Teutonic religion of fire, sword, and swastika.

The Eckart Connection

Dietrich Eckart

Dietrich Eckart was the main figure of the Thule Society. He considered himself the mentor of Adolf Hitler. Some people believe that it was Eckart who suggested to Hitler the use of the swastika as the symbol of the Nazi movement.

Eckart was the editor of a racist periodical, *Auf gut Deutsch* (In Plain German), in which he published articles showing his fascination with German mythology, runic mysteries and the swastika.

An occultist as well as a rabid nationalist, Eckart and a group of the Society's inner circle had been waiting for the appearance of a German messiah who would fuse politics and religion into an unholy crusade against the ideals of the Christian world.

As he lay dying in Munich in December of 1923, Dietrich Eckart's last words were:

"Follow Hitler! He will dance, but it is I who have called the tune! Do not mourn for me: I have influenced history more than any other German."

The Runes Connection

According to another theory, the Nazi swastika is just the result of two superimposed sigel runes, one standing vertically and the other horizontally, as depicted above. The sigel is a rune roughly equivalent to the letter "S," later displayed by the infamous SS.

The photograph on the left, taken in the late twenties, is from the annual commemoration of the Munich beer-hall putsch. The survivors of the debacle, lead by Hitler himself, reenacted every year their march to the Feldherrnhalle. Wreaths were then laid at the tombs of the 16 martyrs of the Nazi movement.

The banners show the typical sinis-troverse Nazi swastika standing on one of its angles. On the lower part of the banners are depicted some "Aryan" sigel runes.

Moreover, the swastika, in different forms, has been commonly found associated with archeological artifacts depicting runes.

Some scholars believe that a precursor of the swastika is the so-called Wolf Cross. Another swastika-like design associated with the swastika is the Dragon Eye, an old Germanic rune in the form of an angular sinistroverse trisquelion. The Ginfaxi, an old Icelandic rune, shows the typical design of a multi-legged sinistroverse swastika.

The picture on the left shows a large runic stone bearing an inscription concerning the dead man it commemorates, three interlocked drinking horns, and a sinistroverse swastika. It was found at Snoldelev, Denmark.

The iron spearhead on the right, showing runic inscriptions and two closed meandroid swastikas, was found at Brest-Litovsk, Russia, probably of Gothic origin, and dated from approximately the Third, the Fourth, or perhaps even the Fifth century B. C. Swastikas, mostly in its sinistroverse form, but also in its dextroverse form, are currently found in ancient weapons.

The Jahn Connection

Many years before the Nazis adopted it, the the swastika had appeared in the monogram of the Turneschaft, a German Gymnastics Society founded in 1811 by the agitator Friedrich Ludwig Jahn, one of the early organizers of the Freikorps.

In 1819, Jahn came under suspicion for his fervent nationalism and strong influence on youth. He was arrested and imprisoned for almost a year; his gymnastic club closed, and a national ban was placed on gymnastics.

Friedrich Jahn

The swastika-like monogram of the Turneschaft, as shown in this coin, was formed out of four "Fs" opposed and joined by their bases, initials of the Society's motto: "Frisch, Frei, Frölisch et Fromm," meaning "Hardy, Free, Cheerful and God-fearing."

The swastika-like design is similar to a kruckenkreuz, formed of two superimposed swastikas, a dextroverse and a sinistroverse one.

The Blavatsky Connection

Helena Blavatsky

Helena Petrovna Blavatsky was a Russian clairvoyant and medium, founder of the Theosophical Society and writer of several books on occultism, among them *Isis Unveiled* and *The Secret Doctrine*. While visiting New York, she met Colonel Henry Steel Scott, a writer for the New York *Daily Graphic*. This was the beginning of a long association. In 1875 Scott and Blavatsky organized the Theosophical Society. The Society grew rapidly and soon after became international.

Mme. Blavatsky's mystic brooch shows her initials in a hexagram topped by a short-legged sinistroverse swastika standing on one of its angles and enclosed in a circle formed by a snake biting its tail —and ancient symbol of infinity.

Some people have speculated that, while living in Vienna, Hitler became interested in the occult, read some theosophist texts and saw the swastika in their literature.

The Karl May Connection

Karl May

Hitler often mentioned that the American Indians used the swastika as a symbol, as he had read about it in stories by Karl May, a German who wrote about the American "Wild West."

As a boy, Hitler liked to read about American cowboys and Indians. He was particularly found of the adventure stories of Karl May, a German who wrote about the American frontier but never visited the United States.

May in "Western" costume

When Hitler became a chancellor he had a special shelf built in his library to hold, in a place of honor, the whole collection of May's novels, specially bound in vel-lum. It is known that Hitler read and reread May's stories and highly com-mended them to his associates and friends.

Some authors believe that it was in Karl May's books where Hitler became infatuated with the Swastika. The swastika was used by many North American Indians, and it frequently appeared in illustrations of May's novels.

The Hanussen Connection

Erik Jan Hanussen

The Weimar Republic — that period of German history that occurred between the departure of the Kaiser and the arrival of Hitler— produced a large and colorful collection of prophets. Prominent among them was Erik Jan Hanussen.

Late in 1930, Hanussen switched completely to prophecy. He became the lodestar for thousands of Germans. Hanussen's followers included an array of Nazi officials. Among them was Karl Ernst, the commander of the Berlin Storm Troopers, and Edmund Heines, an S. A. Gruppenführer. There was also Count von Helldorf, one of the leaders of the local Brownshirts with Ernst. These Nazis, and dozens of others like them, mingled with Hanussen's elite patrons as well as with the film and theater starlets who provided additional entertainment.

Gradually, his prophecies took a distinct Nazi coloring, subtly pushing the cause of the National Socialists. It is known that, at the peak of his Nazi influence, he recommended the adoption of the swastika as an "Indian luck symbol," and indicated that its wearers would be blessed by good fortune.

Hanussen and some of his followers during a seance

Hanussen with Hitler

Hanussen was originally introduced to Hitler by Heinrich Hoffman, the Führer's private photographer, who was also to become the sponsor of Eva Braun. Some authors claim that Hanussen gave Hitler lessons in public speaking, and that Hanussen's coaching was responsible for Hitler's demonic oratory style. It is also said that Hanussen persuaded Hitler to adopt the swastika as the Nazi symbol.

Hanussen also created several horoscopes for the Nazi Party and for Hitler himself.

The Ostara Connection

In 1893, at the age of 19, Lanz von Liebenfels became a novice at a monastery of the Cistercian order on the Austro-Hungarian border, but was expelled six years later. Shortly after being expelled, he founded his Order of the New Templars, which had a strong racial orientation. It was inspired, as the name suggests, by the Templar knights. In 1905 Lanz became the editor and publisher of the anti-Semite magazine *Ostara*.

Adolf Joseph Lanz
von Liebenfels

Named after the ancient Germanic goddess of Spring, *Ostara* was a grotesque, racially motivated magazine devoted to the diffusion of Lanz's ideas. It prominently displayed a double, superposed swastika as a rallying symbol. Most of the ideology of German racial superiority advanced by the Thule Society and later by the Nazis was but a development of the theses published in *Ostara*.

Lanz's notorious magazine attracted Hitler in his early days as an impoverish artist in Vienna. It is known that Hitler was so inflamed with the wild occult, racial, and anti-Semitic theories he found in *Ostara*, that he paid a visit to the editor's offices and came face-to-face with Lanz himself.

Some people claim that it was through the pages of *Ostara* that Hitler became so inflamed by the swastika that he decided to use it as a symbol of the Arian people.

The Thule Connection

Rudolf von Sebottendorf

The Thule Society (Thule Gesselschaft), the real inspiration of Nazism, was founded in August 1919, in Munich, as an off-shoot itself of the Germanen Order. It was created by a strange character named Baron Rudolf von Sebottendorf. Among its most important members were also Max Amann, Anton Drexler, Dietrich Eckart, Hans Frank, Rudolf Hess, Alfred Rosenberg, Gottfried Feder, and others who later became Nazi leaders. Adolf Hitler belonged to the Society as an "associate" or "visiting brother."

In the name of the Thule Gessellschaft, Sebottendorf bought the newspaper *Völkischer Beobachter* — which later became the official Nazi Party journal. Dietrich Eckart, for many years Hitler's mentor, provided the money for the purchase.

Inspired by Madame Blavatsky, he brought to life the age-old myth of Atlantis, calling it Thule. Occultists believe that that Thule, like Atlantis, was the center of a vanished civilization whose members had magic powers.

The emblem of the Thule Society depicted a German dagger over a sinistroverse swastika of curved legs inscribed in a circle.

The Tibetan Connection

Swastika on a Tibetan door as a talisman of good luck

the Nazis' interest in Tibet is well known. The Ahnenerbe, or Nazi Society for Ancestral Heritage, organized several expeditions to Tibet. Their purpose was to locate the origins of the "Nordic" race which was, according to the Nazi theoreticians, of Indo-Germanic stock.

But others contend that the main goal of these expeditions was to get in touch with the spiritual "power-plant" producer of Vril.

From 1926 to 1943 the Nazis sent yearly official SS expeditions to Tibet. In the latter half of the previous century, intriguing hints about Tibetan secret teachings had been carried to the West by Helena Blavatsky, who claimed initiation at the hands of the holy lamas themselves. More to the point, Blavatsky taught that her "Hidden Masters" and "Secret Chiefs" had their earthly residence in the Himalayan region. When the Nazi movement had sufficient funds, it began to organize a number of expeditions to Tibet and these succeeded one another practically without interruption until 1943.

But some people believe that one of the most evident expressions of Nazi interest in Tibet was the party's adoption of Tibet's most important mystical symbol: the swastika.

The Schuler Connection

One of the most important figures in the Völkisch movement at the turn of the century was the mythologist and visionary Alfred Schuler. According to some of his friends, Schuler was literally obsessed with the Swastika. Some of them have mentioned that, during his shamanic trances, he would chant the word "Swastika" like a mantra in an ecstasy of abandonment to the "chthonic" forces that he had summoned.

Alfred Schuler

It has also been repeatedly stated by scholars who specialize in early 20th Century German life and letters, that the young Adolf Hitler was an initiate of Schuler. It is known that both Hitler and Schuler attended the evening gatherings held at the home of Elsa Bruckmann, a Romanian princess and Hitler admirer.

Moreover, it seems that Hitler's wild oratorical style, beginning in a soft and subtly modulated style that suddenly "erupted" into a volcanic frenzy as he seemed to be seized by some demonic force, were a faithful copy of Schuler's lectures, who was described as verbal "orgiastics."

Part Ten
Evolution of the Nazi Swastika

The Evolution of the Nazi Swastika

The Nazi flag was red, with a black sinistroverse swastika inscribed on a white circle and lying on an angle to produce an even more dynamic illusion of circular movement. It took some time, however, until it was fully adopted as the official Nazi symbol. When Adolf Hitler was appointed chief of propaganda for the National Socialist Party in 1920, he realized that the party needed a powerful symbol to identify it and distinguish it from rival groups.

In Nazi theory, the Aryans were the German's ancestors, and Hitler concluded that the swastika, which had been "eternally anti-Semitic," would be the perfect symbol for "the victory of the Aryan man.'" The swastika flag proved to be a dramatic one, and it produced a hypnotic effect on the masses.

The Ehrhardt Brigade arrives in Berlin in this truck marked with a dextroverse swastika lying flat on its side

January 1923. First Nazi rally in Munich. The most interesting thing in this photograph is that at that early date apparently there was no agreement about the type of swastika to use as a Nazi symbol. Even though all of them are sinistroverse, the flags show most swastikas laying flat on one side and also a short-legged swastika, but none of them resting on an angle, like the one later chosen by Hitler.

"This hand guides the Reich: German youth, follow it in the ranks of the Hitler Youth." This late-1920s poster on the left shows the Nazi banner with sinistroverse swastikas standing on its angles, inscribed not in a circle but in a square.

The poster on the right, published in the early thirties by the Communist Party, denounces Hitler: "Workers, how much longer will you allow this comedy to go on? Make an end of it, vote Communist." It depicts Hitler sporting a short-legged dextroverse swastika on his lapel.

1938. Sturmabteilung (SA) thugs defaced Jewish businesses with short-legged swastikas.

"The March into the Grave," a caricature by A. Paul Weber illustrating Ernst Niekisch's 1932 pamphlet *Hitler —ein deutsches Verhängnis* (Hitler, Germany's doom), which predicted that the Nazis would lead Germany to a disaster.

Apparently at this time there was still some confusion about the Nazi symbol. The drawing shows a short-legged sinistroverse swastika standing flat on one of its legs.

Foto on the left shows Hitler attending a rally in Potsdam on 2 October 1932. Behind him there is a large flag depicting the swastika inscribed in a square, not in a circle. Still no agreement!

In 1926, SA leader Ernst Röhm sported in his uniform a flat-lying sinistroverse swastika, but with curved legs. It seems, however, that later somebody manipulated the image to show a correct conventional Nazi swastika.

Part Eleven
Enigmas of
the Swastika

There are several enigmatic things about the swastika that defy a logical explanation

First Enigma

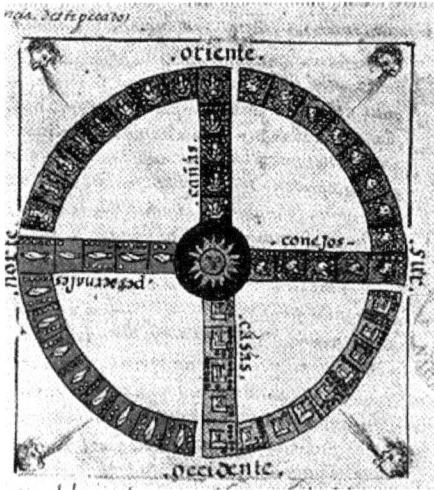

Aztec calendar

Thule Society poster

There is an amazing similarity between the Aztec calendar on the left and the symbol of the Nazi Thule society depicted on the right. Both of them show a perfect circular-shaped swastika. The main difference is that the Nazi swastika is sinistroverse and the Aztec is dextroverse

.

Second Enigma

In 1925 the Kuna Indians of Panamá revolted, slaughtered their panamanian guards, and founded the independent republic of Thule. Its new flag had a swastika on an orange background with a red border. The Republic existed for several years.

A primary focus of Thule-Gesellschaft (Thule Secret Society), one of the roots of the Nazi movement, was a claim concerning the origins of the Aryan race, which they believed was in a mythical land called Thule, located in the furthest north. There is no explanation as to how the Kuna established the connection with Thule and the swastika.

Third Enigma

The Basque swastika, also called Labaru by the Spanish Basque and Croix a Virgule by the French Basque because it resembles four commas, is believed to be unique. It is not found in any other place in Europe, Asia, or America. How can we explain, then, the presence of this perfect Basque sinistroverse swastika on the lid of this small, round box made out of birchbark, wood, and porcupine quills by the Mimac Indians of Nova Scotia?

The box is at the McCord Museum in Montreal.

Fourth Enigma

The swastika as a symbol of fertility and life

By some natives in the Amazon

By the early Greeks

The terracota cover, "tanga" on the left is from the Caneotires river, Brazil. The bronze statuette depicting the goddess Astarté was found by Schliemann during excavations at the site of Troy.

How two different cultures in such two far apart places assigned the same symbolism to the swastika is difficult to explain.

Fifth Enigma

Aztec painted codex

Maya engraving on rock

Engraving on rock. Tiahuanacu. Peru

The zooorphic swastika on the left is made out of 4 feathered serpents representing the Aztec god Quetzalcoátl. The one on the center represents the Maya god Kukulkán with two overlapping swastikas in the background. The one on the right is from the ruins in Tiahuanacu, Peru, with four serpents most likely representing the god Viracocha. They are all the same god. According to the legend, Quetzalcoátl-Kukulkán-Viracocha, came from outer space —planet Venus.

Sixth Enigma

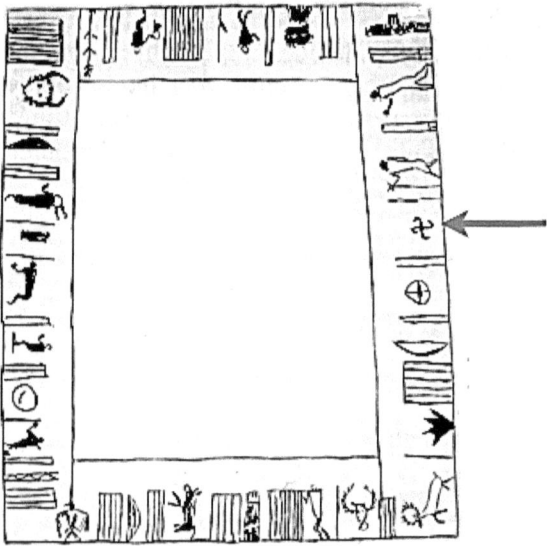

Tibetan & Kansa Indians divination diagrams. The Kansa Indians lived along the Kansas and Saline rivers in what is now central Kansas, United States. How both of them used swastikas on their divination diagrams and placed them almost in the same location?

Part Twelve
The Swastika:
A Cosmic Symbol?

After so many years of studying this symbol I have concluded that the swastika is a cosmic symbol. Adding to the fact that most of the early cultures who used the swastika as a symbol had a strong fixation with "gods" from above, I base my theory on two things:

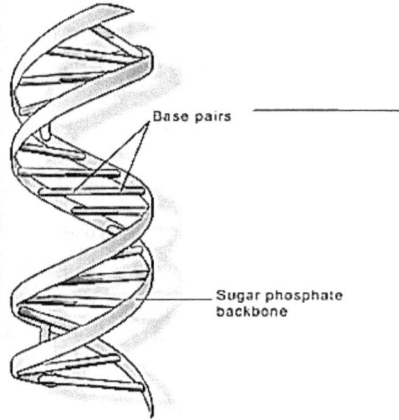

In 1953 American biologist James Watson and English Physicist Francis Crick discovered the structure of the DNA molecule —the basis of life in this planet. The DNA molecule is shaped like a double helix.

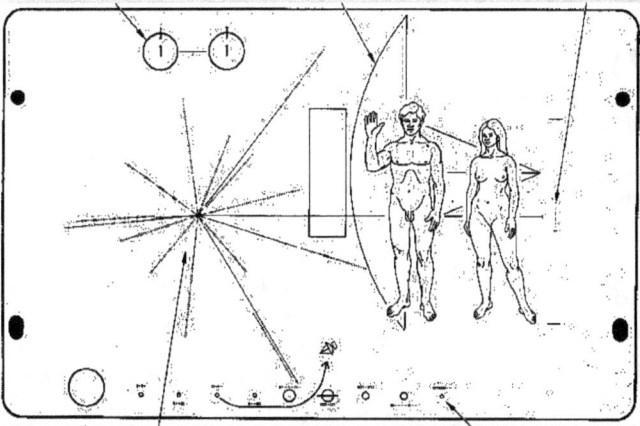

In 1972 we sent a message to the cosmos. The message was printed on a 6 by 9 inch gold-anodized aluminum plate and sent to the space by NASA on a Pioneer spacecraft. The message contained information about life on planet earth, its position on the solar system and the nature of the spacecraft.

Two years later, on November, 1974, we sent another message to the cosmos, this one from the Arecibo Observatory in Puerto Rico. This message (below on the left) was a pseudo-digital one, using two different radio frequencies to represent "0" and "1." A visual representation of the message (on the right) shows that it included a representation of the DN molecule, the most accurate representation of life in this planet.

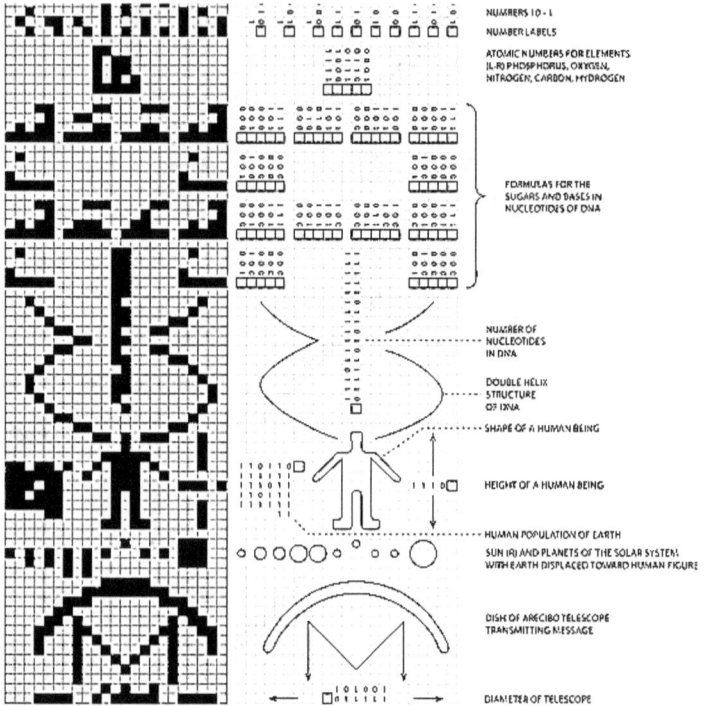

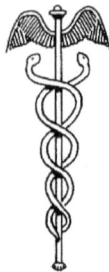

But it seems that some people knew about the DNA molecule way before Watson & Crick's discovery.

According to the Greek myth, while walking on the countryside, Hermes, the god of merchants and robbers, found two serpents, and he picked them up with his walking staff. The staff with the serpents eventually became the caduceus, a Greek symbol of medicine and life.

Actually, the ancient Greek's caduceus is actually a rough representation of the double helix of the DNA molecule.

Some years ago I reached the conclusion that the swastika is a representation of the DNA molecule. Though author David Icke has recently mentioned the relation between the caduceus and the DNA molecule, I already had mentioned it in my multimedia program: *The Riddle of the Swastika: A Study in Symbolism*, published in 1993 and registered at Apple computer.

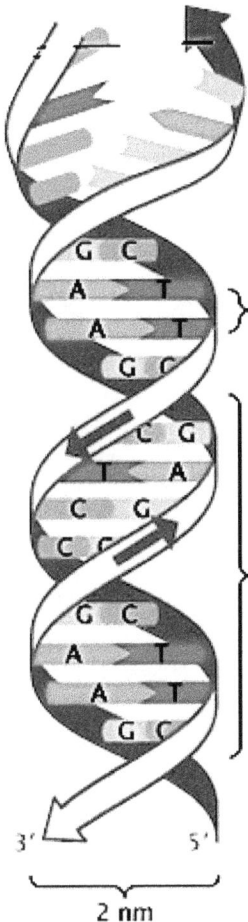

The DNA, as first described by Watson and Crick, is a right-handed helix closely resembling a dextroverse sigmoidean swastika. Normal B-DNA, normally occurs as two separate long polymers ("strands") that wrap around each other in a helical spiral around an imaginary helix axis. If you view the DNA from end on, you will see only a tight circle of atoms. The helix axis would be in the center of this circle. In what direction do the DNA strands spiral away from you around the helix axis?

The normal form of DNA is exclusively a right-handed helix. This is determined by the overall stability of the stacking interactions, which favor right-handed helices. Some scientists believe that the DNA's exclusively right-hand twist is one of the central pieces of evidence that indicates a single origin of all life on planet Earth and probably on the whole universe.

Epilogue

The Swastika Belongs to Mankind

The author at the entrance of the Philadelphia Museum of Art

It seems that, after the Nazis misappropriated the swastika and put it to their evil use, they contaminated this symbol forever. For more than half a century they have had this symbol hostage. Most people all around the world still believe that the swastika only symbolizes Nazism.

But, as we have seen, the swastika had a long life before Hitler and the Nazis. It has been for centuries a symbol of laughter, joy and good luck. It is one of the oldest symbols of mankind. Its Nazi connections are only a speck in its very long existence. It is a symbol that deserves a better treatment from history.

Should Christians renounce to the use of the cross as their main symbol just because the Ku Klux Klan has used it? Of course not!

Leaving the swastika in the hands of the Nazis is the worst disservice we can do to the Indians of North, Central and South America. Moreover, it is offensive to the people of Tibet, Nepal, China, India and Japan. It is disrespectful to the Basque, the French, the Irish, the Ashanti, the Ethiopians, the Iranians, the Jordanians, the Sicilians, the Estonians, the Latvians, the Finnish and many other peoples around the world.

Industrial designer Henry Dreyfuss once wrote:

"The fact that an ignominious fanatic placed a swastika on his battle flag is insufficient reason for ignoring this symbol's historic significance."

The time is ripe to rescue this beautiful and enigmatic symbol from under Nazi control and bring it to the place it deserves among other similar symbols in the long history of mankind.

Please, join me in this search and rescue mission of the swastika.

Bibliography

Bibliography

Alleau, Rene, *Hitler et les societes secretes*. Paris: Grasset, 1969.
Angebert, Jean-Michel, *Hitler et les religions de swastika*. Paris: Robert Laffont, 1969.
—— *Les mystiques du soleil*. Paris 1971.
—— *The Occult and the Third Reich*. NewYork: 1974.
Argüelles, Miriam and José, *The Feminine*. Boulder, Colorado: Shambala, 1977.
Baird, Jay W., *The Mythical World of Nazi Propaganda, 1939-1944*. Minneapolis: 1975.
Bertrand, Louis, *Adolf Hitler*. Paris: 1936.
Brennan, J. H., *The Occult Reich*. New York: 1974.
Brissaud, Andre, *Hitler et l'ordre noir*. Paris: Librairie academique Perrin, 1969.
Brown, William Norman, *The Swastika, a study of the Nazi claims of its Aryan origin*. New York: Emerson Books, Inc., [1933].
Butts, Edward, *The Swastika*. Kansas City: Franklin Hudson, 1921.
Carr, Joseph, *The Twisted Cross*. Shreveport, Louisiana: Huntington House, 1985.
Carrera Justiz, Francisco, *El urbanismo prehistórico: los arios, la swastika, Troya*. La Habana: Imprenta Cuba Intelectual, 1945.
Conquerwood, Charles R., *The Moral of two German marks*. Montreal: 1942.
Davis, Renee, *La Croix gammee, cette enigme*. Paris: Presses de la Citte, 1967.
Dahlke, Rüdiger, *Mandalas the World*. New York: Sterling, 1992.
Eco, Umberto, *A Theory of Semiosis*. Bloomington, Indiana: Indiana University Press, 1979.
Frère, Jean-Claude, *Nazisme et societes secretes*. Paris: Grasset, 1974
Goblet d'Alviella, E., *La croix gammé ou swastika*. Paris, 1891.
Goodrick-Clarke, Nicholas, *The Occult Roots of Nazism*. Wellingborough: Aquarium Press, 1985.
Godwin, Joscelyn, *Arktos. The Polar Myth in Science, Symbolism, and Nazi Survival*. Grand Rapids, MI: Phanes Press, 1993.
Halle, Morris, et al., *Semiosis: Semiotics and the History of Culture*. The University of Michigan, 1984.
Hanfstaengl, Ernst, *Hitler: les annés obscures*. Paris: Trevise, 1967.
Hayes, Will, *The Swastika: A Study in Comparative Religion*. Chatham, England: The Order of the Great Companion, 1934.
Heller, Steven, *The Swastika: Symbol Beyond Redemption?* New York; Allworth Press, 2000.

Howard, Michael, The Occult Conspiracy. New York: MJF Books, 1989

King, Francis, *Satan and Swastika*. St. Albans: Mayflower, 1976.

Langer, Walter G., *The Mind of Adolph Hitler*. New York: Basic Books, 1972.

Levenda, Peter, *Unholly Alliance: A History of Nazi Involvement with the Occult*. New York: Avon, 1995.

Lowenstein, John Prince, *The Swastika: Its History and Meaning*. London: Royal Anthropological Institute, 1941.

ManWoman, *Gentle Swastika*. Cranbrook, British Columbia: Flyfoot Press, 2001.

Marillier, Bernard, *Le Svastika*. Puiseaux, France: Pardes, 1997.

Milloué, Louis de, *Le Swastika*. In Annales du Musée Guimet, Vol, 31, Paris, 1909.

Ortiz, Fernando, *El huracán, su mitología y sus símbolos*. México, FCE, 1947.

Pauwels, Louis, and Jacques Bergier, *The Morning of the Magicians*. New York: Avon Books, 1971.

Peirce, Charles Sanders, *Peirce on Signs* (edited by James Hoopes), Chapel Hill, N.C.: Univ. Of Carolina Press, 1991.

Peirce, Charles Sanders, *Philosophical Writings of Peirce*. New York: Dover, 2011.

Pennik, Nigel, *The Swastika*. Cambridge: Fenris-Wolf, 1979.

Petittrere, Ray, *La Mystique de la croix Gammee*. Paris: Editions France-Empire, 1962.

Quinn, Malcolm, *The Swastika: Constructing the Symbol*. New York: Routledge, 1997.

Ravenscroft, Trevor, *The Spear of Destiny*. New York: Putnam's, 1974.

Roberts, J. M., *The Mythology of the Secret Societies*. St. Albans: 1974.

Rosio, Bob, *Hitler and the New Age*. Lafayette, Louisiana: Huntington House, 1993

Scheuerman, Wilhelm, *Woher kommt das Hakenkreuz*. Berlin: Kowolt Verlag, 1933.

Sebeok, Thomas A., *I Think I Am a Verb: More Contributions to the Doctrine of Signs*. New York: Plenum, 1986.

Simons, Tom, "Why is DNA right-handed? UNL finding supports hypothesis," *Nebraska Today*, 9/17/214, https://news.unl.edu/newsrooms/unltoday/article/why-is-dna-right-handed-unl-finding-supports-hypothesis/

Sklar, Dusty, *The Nazis and the Occult*. New York: Dorset Press, 1977.

Taylord, Telford, *Sword and Swastika*. London, 1953.

Urueta, Chano, *La swastika de Adolfo*. Monterrey, N. L., Nexico: 1941.

Waite, Robert G. L., *The Psychopathic God. Adolf Hitler*. New York: Signet Books, 1977.

Walker, Norman. *Real History of the Swastika*. London: Lutherford, 1939.

Webb, James, *The Occult Establishment*. La Salle, Il.: Open Court, 1976.

Wilson, Thomas, *The Swastika*. Washington, D.C.: Smithsonian Institution, 1896.

Wulff, Wilhelm, *Zodiac and Swastika*. New York: Coward, McCann & Geoghegan, 1973.

Other books by Servando Gonzalez

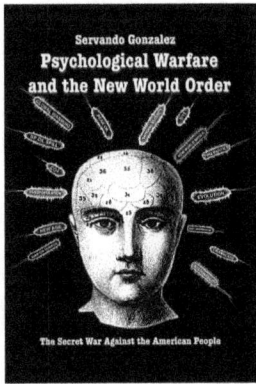

Psychological Warfare and the New World Order: The Secret War Against the American People

America is at war. But this not a conventional war waged with tanks, battleships and planes in conventional battlefields —at least not yet. It is a secret, insidious type of war whose battleground is the people's minds. Its main weapons are propaganda and mass brainwashing by disin-formation, cunning, deception and lies in a large scale not used against the people of any nation since Nazi Germany. Though important, however, those elements are just part of a series of carefully planned and executed long and short-term psychological warfare operations. In synthesis, it is a psychological war —a PsyWar.

If an unfriendly foreign power had carried out against the American people the actions carried out by Wall Street bankers, Oil magnates and CEOs of transnational corporations entrenched at the Council on Foreign Relations and its parasite organizations, we might well have considered it an act of war. Unfortunately, most Americans ignore that they are under attack. The reason is because, like Ninja assassins, the main weapon used by the conspirators who have managed to infiltrate and take control of the U.S. Government and most of American life has been their invisibility. For almost a century, these small group of conspirators have been waging a quiet, non-declared war of attrition against the American people, and it seems that they are now ready for the final, decisive battle.

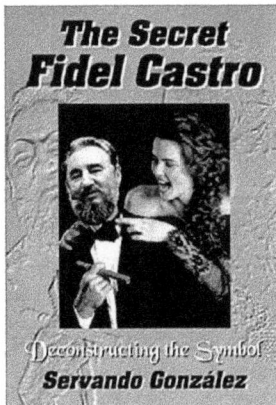

The Secret Fidel Castro : Deconstructing the Symbol

Ths neither a history of the Cuban revolution nor a biography of Fidel Castro. The book follows what intelligence services call a CPP (short for Comprehensive Personality Profile), similar to the ones intelligence services keep on foreign leaders. It focuses on different aspects of Castro?s actions and personality which, for some reasons, have been either ignored, misunderstood, or misrepresented. The main thesis of this book is that there are many different Castros.

The most widely known is the symbolic, public one, as it has been portrayed in official Cuban propaganda, Castro-friendly biographies, and mainstream American media. But there are also many secret Castros, highly different from the public one.

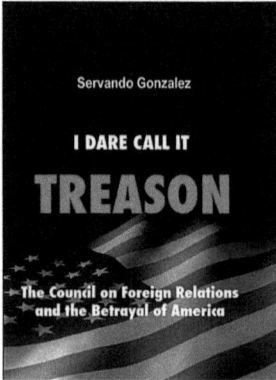

I Dare Call It Treason: The Council on Foreign Relations and the Betrayal of America

Servando Gonzalez

I DARE CALL IT

TREASON

The Council on Foreign Relations and the Betrayal of America

The Council on Foreign Relations (CFR) describes itself as a sort of social club where the rich and powerful get together to discuss national and international politics from a rational, non-partisan, patriotic perspective. But, really, what is the Council on Foreign Relations? The CFR is many things. It is a millionaires club, a communo-fascist party in power, an intelligence agency, a think tank, a criminal gang, an association of assassins and mass murderers, a cabal of sociopaths and psychopaths, a sect involved in the occult and a pirates' den.

The CFR is the visible head of the Invisible Government of the United States. Its core nucleus is composed of international bankers, oil magnates and CEOs of transnational corporations. But, most importantly, the CFR is the true axis of evil in the world. The CFR's main enemy is the people of the world, particularly the American people. This explains why, behind every single act of treason against the American people, you can always find, hiding in the shadows, one or more members of the Council on Foreign Relations.

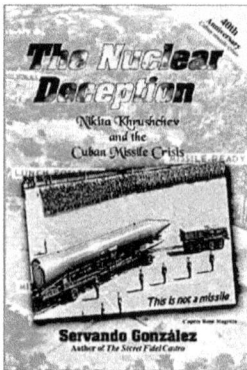

The Nuclear Deception

Nikita Khrushchev and the Cuban Missile Crisis

This is not a missile

Servando González
Author of The Secret Fidel Castro

Cuban Missile Crisis

The event known as the Cuban missile crisis, the greatest of all Cold War crises, is a milestone in the history of the Cold War. Some analysts even have concluded that what was called the Cold War ended in 1962 with the Cuban missile crisis. Yet there is perhaps no single event in recent history as puzzling as this one. There are many questions that still remain unanswered. Why did Khrushchev risk so much? What was his ultimate purpose? Why did he withdraw so fast? Why did he not retaliate at other sensitive points, like Berlin?

Why did President Kennedy not seize the opportunity to get rid of Castro? Why did the Americans permit the shootdown of a U-2 plane over Cuba without taking retaliatory actions? Who shot down the U-2, and under what conditions did it happen? Why did Kennedy allow the Soviet ships to leave Cuba without boarding them, to physically verify that the canvas-covered objects on deck were actually missiles and their nuclear warheads on their way back to the U.S.S.R.? According to the author, the main questions of the crisis have eluded satisfactory answers, because most of the analysts who have studied it have neglected the true Cuban role in the event, and because the fundamental question about the crisis, namely, why Khrushchev installed strategic nuclear missiles in Cuba, has been erroneously formulated. Consequently, it has been impossible to find the right answer to a question, when the question itself is wrong.

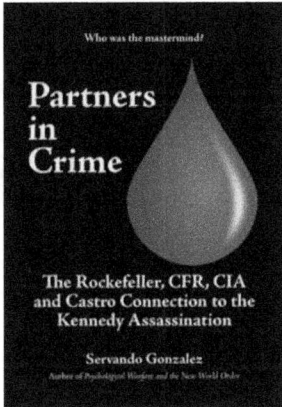

Partners in Crime: The Rockefeller, CFR, CIA and Castro Connection to the Kennedy Assassination

Most books about the assassination of President Kennedy written by "serious" authors and published by "prestigious" publishing houses fully agree with the Warren Commission's conclusions that Lee Harvey Oswald was a mentally disturbed individual who acted alone and there was no conspiracy surrounding him. the few who blame the CIA, usually lefties and "progressives," never mention the key role played by important Council on Foreign Relations'

They also purposely ignore Castro's role in the event, despite the fact that he was the only one among the suspects who publicly threatened the Kennedy brothers with assassination and had a long personal history of violence and a strong inclination to commit such a crime. Moreover, none of these books adds to the list of suspects the man who created the CFR, the CIA and Castro: David Rockefeller.

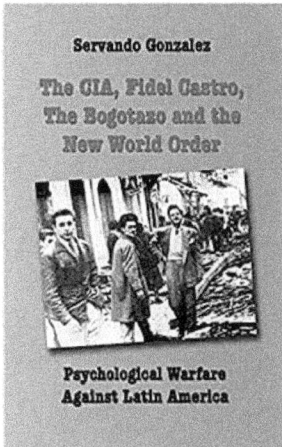

The CIA, Fidel Castro, The Bogota and the New World Order. Psychological Warfare Against Latin America

On April 9, 1948, Bogotá, the capital of Colombia, was the scene of violent riots that later became known as the Bogotazo. The event that apparently triggered the riots was the assassination of Colombian leader Jorge Eliécer Gaitán. Participants in the riot destroyed most of the city center. Several thousand people were killed.

The riots coincided with the celebration in the city of the Ninth Pan American Conference of Foreign Ministers, which had opened its sessions a few days earlier, on March 30.

The riots coincided with the celebration in the city of the Ninth Pan American Conference of Foreign Ministers, which had opened its sessions a few days earlier, on March 30. The Conference was presided over by General George Marshall, U.S. Secretary of State. Marshall, like John Foster Dulles, who succeeded him, was a lawyer in a Wall Street firm and a senior executive of the Council on Foreign Relations. In reality, the Bogotazo was not a spontaneous explosion of popular violence, but a false flag operation that initiated in the Western Hemisphere a large-scale psychological warfare operation later known as the Cold War.

Intelligence and Espionage: A Game with no Rules

Espionage has been called the second oldest profession, and has lately become one of the newest fields of scholarly study. More than forty American colleges and universities offer courses in espionology (the study of intelligence and espionage). Several private institutions are dedicated to the advance of espionology and encourage an "the study of the history, organization, and methods of intelligence", in colleges and universities, and work to improve public understanding of the role of intelligence in national security.

So, just out of curiosity, let's take an open-minded close look at this irreverent book on the second oldest profession. I am sure you are going to like it. Real-life spy stories are much more interesting than any spy book written by John Le Carré, Len Deighton, Robert Ludlum or Tom Clancy ... and, similar to what we have read in these highly entertaining novels, most of "true" spy stories are pure fiction, that is, pure bovine manure!

www.ingramcontent.com/pod-product-compliance
Lightning Source LLC
Chambersburg PA
CBHW072144020426
42334CB00018B/1878